The Universe of
Little Beaver Lake

poems by

Laurie Higi

Finishing Line Press
Georgetown, Kentucky

The Universe of
Little Beaver Lake

ACKNOWLEDGMENTS

The following poems have been published:
"Open to your Dew" *Confluence Literary Magazine*
"Canada in Common" *Confluence Literary Magazine*
"More Vulnerable than Me" *Surreal Beauty Magazine*
"Butterflies and Empty Books" *The Dandelion Review*

Thank you to George and all of my peers in poetry. For your guidance, I am
eternally grateful.

Publisher: Leah Maines
Editor: Christen Kincaid
Cover Art: Michelle Marqueling
Author Photo: Kaytlin Higi
Cover Design: Elizabeth Maines McCleavy

Printed in the USA on acid-free paper.
Order online: www.finishinglinepress.com
             also available on amazon.com

Author inquiries and mail orders:
Finishing Line Press
P. O. Box 1626
Georgetown, Kentucky 40324
U. S. A.

Table of Contents

Dedicated to the Stringfield Family
Thank you for giving me Canada

Section I.
Hidden Stars

Medians of Wildflowers

I see a sign for Gibraltar
On the way to Ontario.
My interest is peaked.
I knew that I would write.
The trickle of words is starting
To flow through the wet that I bleed.

Four hours he has been telling me
That he loves me.
I know that he expects some reply.
My silence is no good.

I pay close attention to medians of wildflowers.
Lightning passing like fish through my window.
I dream of crossing the bridge border
To the world of stars,
The universe of words that has not yet come.

Four more hours of anticipation, silence.
Then,
Five days of inspiration,
Explosions.

This Side of My Childhood

Life has brought me back
To this side of
Innocence.
From this window
I can see how drastically
Things have changed.

One thing
That has remained brings
These words.
Stars that flow
From mouth to paper.
Brings me this explosion of green light
Canada.
Makes me yearn for past fire.

You don't where I am

                        Now.

Now that these words
                    Pour
From my brain,   out my ear
             To this anxious hand,
Even in a place as obscure as
                    Canada.

I've searched a thesaurus to grasp
The word that describes us.
The only word
In my head floats into the black sky
                        With the sparks
                              Of this bonfire.

I Can't Hear the Flowers

Every morning, night,
Cigarette, this screened-
In porch looking out
On the lake, flowers,
The cornucopia of words
I am craving.

But the transparent walls are keeping
Canada out, and I am terrified
To tear it down
And let my pen scribble
Anything but the answers
To this book of crossword puzzles.

This porch is more than
A mosquito net, more than
A sun block.
I can't hear the flowers
From my perch on this plastic lawn chair,
Only the sound of my coffee
Getting cold, and the taste
Of my smoke going out.

Butterflies and Empty Books

This cornucopia is crammed
Full of butterflies and empty
Books. I try to make space
By filling the books with ink.

I am careful not to pull
Wings off of butterflies,
Though part of me wants so bad
To examine them. Find words
To describe, in these empty books,
Every color, spot, line antenna.

Maybe tattoo it on my fingernail,
The one that I see with.
Put it next to the star,
The fire, the fish, and the lake
Named after a beaver.

Hidden Stars

A country road that neither wheel nor foot has touched;
A fishing pole sitting on a dock with a line;
A pillow on which no hair will ever rest;
A cold lake on which ice is afraid to crystalize.

Waiting stars hidden by the full moon;
The big dipper is pulsing with suspense.
Though my mind can take it all in,
What emerges are only these simple words.

From these docks, from these roads,
Only this.

I arrive.
Little Beaver Lake is
An infinite puddle
Of Canada for me
To drink up with my ear,
Eye.

I am but a fish
Caught on the hook of its line.

Laughing Like My Inner Child

We jump into Little Beaver Lake,
as refreshing as watermelon Jolly Ranchers.

A goose bump of fish passes my leg.
26-year old children living
this childhood we never had together.
Held up by grandkids' inflatable dinosaurs.

I laugh like my inner child as seaweed tickles
my leg, foot, toe. You scream and cry
like a scared adult, over-thinking it. Kicking over to you,
out-of-breath smile on my face.
The long green plants
I cannot see try to hold me back,
pull me down. I keep kicking.

Now, my back burning, I reach your hand, and pull
you out of weed. I talk you through it between gulps
of air and breaths of water.
Clear water greets us like a cool breeze on a dog day.
You are still an adult and I have dirt under my fingernails
and a Kool Aid mustache.

A Mussel in the Shape of a Zebra

As the men fish all day
In Little Beaver Lake,
I wade up to my thighs,
Worrying for a moment
That the zebra mussels will latch
Onto my toe.
Then, I worry that I'll never see one.
Like never knowing what could be.
A mussel in the shape of a zebra,
Or the color of that old TV screen
We've been examining late at night?
Maybe neither, though I lean
On the second. I could be
                                        Right.

When the moon makes the lake
Cold, I sit in this little cabin
Kitchen, after zebra mussels
Are asleep, and wonder,
Why are we eating
Fish instead of stars?

Mosquitoes to Our Light

Starlight stretches over Little Beaver
Lake. The only light, our bonfire, crackling like ice
On the first day of spring.
Two guitars and one voice attracting neighbors

Like mosquitoes to our light.
Instead of swatting them away I walk down to the dock,
This wobbling wood erected years before
And lay flat on my back to take in
The stars that are falling to me like fireflies,
Wanting to be caught by my magnificent mouth.

With strings playing through my ear
Lines that I haven't written in months
Come flowing through me like the water,
The stars, the fish, the fire.
They are all mine.

Section II.
I've Stumbled into Stars

Open to Your Dew

I'm starting to grow   out
Of you,
My favorite pair of old jeans
Worn   so   right
Holes appear in all the wrong places.

And   I could kiss you,
Rock of Gibraltar,
My eye a moist clamp,
                    So tight.
My lip   open
                    To your dew.

With all the passion
Of so deeply wishing
                    For something,
Not this amazing Canadian
Summer,   but long winter,
                         Pure   white   snow.

And   I write cut off metaphors
While blaring Led Zeppelin   for inspiration,
Like you,   white trash intellectual.
One minute   cussing like a broken toe,
The next   picking constellations out of Ontario
Night skies   a half a pack of cigarettes
North of Toronto.

Only Window Awake at 4 in the Morning

Covered in sleep and cinnamon
Things that make sense here
Are fantastic when the lid
Of my dream is lifted.

My ear sees this Canada wind
Blow off Little Beaver Lake
Into my window. The only window
Awake at 4 in the morning.

Only window that makes
This picture so passionate
That I feel more love asleep. Only wind
That can bring you, Hoosier son, to Canada.

After dreams of lip, leg, forearm
Undulating through my mind, "I dreamt
Of scarves in turquoise and fuchsia
That said here, here is joy in focus."*

*Quote borrowed from the Lisa Zimmerman poem, "The Wind,
The Lake, The Deer."

Losses, Gains, Stars

I was more impressed
By the ferry ride across the river
Than by The Lake in the Mountain.
Expectations let you down
And beauty sneaks peaks
At you when you are looking away.

This life. Unexpected apologies,
Losses, gains, stars
That seem to shine brighter
When you close your eyes.
Dreaming of how things use to
Look, feel, sound.

The difference of initial beauty,
Enchantment,
Or lack thereof,
And love.

I've Stumbled into Stars

Tongues of fire mixing with strong
Canadian beer, a melody
Licking this soft, green
Canadian silence with American
Acoustics.
Ten fingers burning these
Two guitars. A family
I've stumbled into. Stars
Falling towards us,
So many headlights,
We see millions of years ago
Swimming our direction in one night.

These words,
The music of my mind,
Flowing like the fish
Through the night sky,
Unstoppable, unstopped,
Under stars.

Disappear into Poems

I have my own room here,
26 with little mermaid sheets.
Five days that have become an indistinguishable
Flame of love,
Stars, mixed with fish
And words.

August, the lake is cooling
And the cabin is already bracing for winter.
These goose bumps make
Me want to stay forever
Absorbing the explosions of words
That erupt from me here.

At this moment six feet
Of snow seems manageable
With a little space heater.
Just to write, alone, or on the frozen
Lake. To disappear into poems,
Metaphors. To lay on the dock
And be scooped up by the big dipper.

Mixing With the Quiet

With no sound but our fire crackling
The bull frogs on Little Beaver Lake
This non-quiet that is as silent
As the cathedral on Monday afternoon.

The religious experience we feel
As the energy flows through your
Arm   about my shoulder   and into
My stomach   as you point out shooting
Stars whose flight we hear
As streaming constellations in our bones.

Mixing with the quiet   After years
Of regular strangers   tonight
I know you more than anyone

Section III.
I've Never Ranked Stars with Body Parts

The Beautiful Side of a Maple Leaf

Your apology letter,
Like these Canada poems.
When all is said and   begun,
The words,   metaphors,
Hastily climb back through my ear and into my brain.
After months of quiet as a museum
At midnight,

Now the beautiful side
Of a maple leaf in autumn.
Soul one.
I thought I was paralyzed
By all of these bonfires in my spine,
When Canada poems,
When bonfires,
When apology letters
Can still hold a pen.

Canada in Common

As I write of stars and cinnamon,
The past that I live,
Past that blacks out
The present, mortalizes the future,

You walk in, with Ontario
And independence on my mind,
You talk of your cabin in Toronto.

Canada in common.

You won't let me push you
Away like some dog starved
For attention. Now I don't want to.
My life finally coming together,
The perfect mixture of night,

Day when dusk,
I tear up at the beauty of it.
We talk of Canada. Our own
Canadas collide.

More Vulnerable than Me

The conjugation of soft, comfortable love
Into hunger for old times past.
Where there used to be this incandescent
Glow of everything I ever wanted,
I replace it with this flame
And the peculiar way it wraps
Itself around my neck.
Not choke,
But some other verb.

As I proudly sang of love I knew
Nothing about,
The present extinguisher made this fire
More vulnerable than me
And this verb changed to smoking.

I've Never Ranked Star with Body Part

I haven't felt the tingle
Of the stars through my spine since Canada.
Your hand, my knee,
Squeezing.
I feel like I'll spontaneously combust
If we are not alone.
Me, stars, you,
Your hand, my knee.
I've never ranked star
With body part until now.

Outside your house
Stars look Canadian.
This cold like Canada,
The warmth I thought
Only it could offer.

Infinite Navy Blue Ocean

Today, you showed me
Your Canada. An aerial view.
More evergreen fingers
Reaching towards me,
Pulling me into blue lakes.
Less cabins, intense beauty
Of simplicity.

I can imagine how breath-giving
Night is there.
Completely outshining Ontario
With less light.

Now, after two days of you
I can't scrub your smell
From me.
It shouldn't be hard
To admit that
I love you, today, yesterday,
Last week.

To share Canada with you.
You ask me about these poems,
My brilliant fish,
My secret fire.

You've interrupted this universe
I've created for myself.
You've become the first
To penetrate my skin.

I try to deny that I want you
Here, lying on the dock,
Fingers intertwined
Towards those stars,
Shining fish swimming
Through this infinite
Navy blue ocean.

The Universe of Little Beaver Lake

I received everything
I wanted
Except an aurora borealis.
Maybe I could have handled one,
Mixing with this fire that has engulfed
My eye and my pen.

Stars like fish swimming through my
Incandescent fingers.
Fish like stars flowing out
Of my reach.
So loud that the stars are jealous
Of this universe of Little Beaver Lake.

Thousands of constellations
Thousands of years ago.
The big dipper forms in front of me,
Drying out my pen and
Wetting my eye
With hush   linear explosions.

Laurie Higi writes poetry on her chicken farm in South Whitley, Indiana. She draws inspiration from the sky, love, family, and the amazing, local poetry community. She has a Bachelor of Arts in English Writing from Indiana University- Purdue University, Fort Wayne. Her poetry has appeared in *The Dandelion Review, Confluence Literary Magazine, Surreal Beauty Magazine,* and *Bohemia Art Magazine.* She has also published her work in *Reality Serum Magazine.* She enjoys being surrounded by flowers, clouds, and stars, with her husband and four children, on their farm. In the summertime, she can be found in her garden, weeding, harvesting, and wondering how to incorporate greens beans into a poem. She is a fan of supporting her local economy in any way that she can. She is currently working on writing and compiling another poetry chapbook to share with the world.